CW00545990

all good
things must
~~come to an end~~
start
with BIS
MIL
LAH

TAQDEER

A FAITH AND PSYCHOLOGY
INSPIRED LIFESTYLE BRAND.

A simple, comprehensive Islamic inspired journaling concept cultivating gratitude and happiness through the remembrance of Allah (swt).

CREATED BY S. SAMIA QUDDUS

Published by Deft Group Ltd.
ISBN Number: 978-1-5272-1164-3
Copyright 2021. Deft Group Ltd.
First published 2018 by Deft Group Ltd.
All rights reserved.

Designed by The Grid | www.designthegrid.com

www.taqdeer.life | salaam@taqdeer.life

Ash-Shukr
The Acknowledging One,
The Rewarder of Thankfulness,
The Grateful, The Appreciative.

The One who recognises righteous and good acts, no matter how small. The One who rewards immensely for all acts of obedience, no matter how small. The One who rewards effort, no matter how small. The One who rewards sincere intentions, even if unable to perform.

In the name of Allah,
Most Gracious, Most Merciful

*Welcome to your journey
of Alhamdulillah journaling.*

"If you are grateful, I will give you more."

AL-IBRAHIM : 7

INTRODUCTION

'Taqdeer', which denotes 'appreciation' in Arabic is a comprehensive faith-inspired Islamic gratitude journal that cultivates an Alhamdulillah (praise be to God) mind-set, whilst also developing psychological mindedness. As a qualified Integrative Therapist (MBACP) and mental health advocate, I have attempted to bridge Islamic, scientific and psychotherapeutic principles. This serves as an assurance that what you are about to start will change your life for the better, insha'Allah.

I am largely grateful to my therapist training where I found through research that intrapsychic self-examination (i.e. self-awareness) is consistent with Islamic philosophy[1,2]. In 2017, this finding further spurred on the creation of Taqdeer and a year later Taqdeer was launched.

Over the years, Taqdeer has reached a global audience with the 'Taqdeer Life' family spanning across America, Australia, Belgium, Canada, France, Germany, Holland, India, Malaysia, Norway, Saudi Arabia, Sweden, Switzerland, South Africa, Turkey, Qatar and the UAE, Alhamdulillah.

What has been most encouraging is witnessing Taqdeer's interfaith potential in supporting individuals who originate from other faith backgrounds and are spiritual in nature, also benefiting from the commonalities that exist with faith-based gratitude practices. See Testimonials for commendations received from some members of our Taqdeer Life family.

[1] *Quddus, S. (2020) Trust in Allah, but tie your camel.*
[2] *Kershavarzi H, Haque, A. (2013) Outlining a Psychotherapy Model for Enhancing Muslim Mental Health within an Islamic Context*

This revised edition of Taqdeer is a culmination of feedback gained from the Taqdeer Life family and further personal research. Though noticeably shorter, the journal remains concise and impactful. The multiple different layouts scattered throughout Taqdeer continue to address various aspects of a gratitude mind-set whilst still maintaining the same structure. A detailed introduction is designed to establish an Alhamdulillah mind-set and formulate intention from a scientific/ psychological and spiritual perspective before proceeding with the act of journaling. The content is largely similar to its predecessor with some new features to enhance your journaling experience and develop spiritual practice. These include:

- the transliteration of the morning and evening Adhkar, aimed at emphasising its translation and to encourage daily practise
- a short introduction to Islamic mindfulness 'al-Muraqabah', aimed at improving your connection with Allah (swt)
- an exploration of our values system, aimed at promoting happiness and bettering ourselves
- a bullet journal feature on Notes, Thoughts & Plans pages, aimed at organising thoughts to support your mental health and emotional well-being
- a carefully researched and collated gratitude reference aimed at providing the Taqdeer Life family with thankfulness/Shukr related quotes derived from Quranic verses and spiritual sayings.

The inclusion of an artwork postcard is a unique feature to Taqdeer. As gold now features on our journal cover, this ties in with Taqdeer's most prevalent change; the inclusion of 'Jalla Jalalahu', a beautiful artwork piece created by award winning and contemporary Islamic artist, Ms. Maaida Noor. Jalla Jalalahu encompasses traditional artistic elements. This combined with the use of line and triangular composition creates depth and complements Taqdeer's logo to elicit a contemporary feel.

Ms. Noor's piece exhibits at Cambridge Central mosque alongside other renound Muslim artists from around the world. Thus I am deeply grateful to Ms. Noor for her generosity in allowing Jalla Jalalahu to be featured in Taqdeer, whilst also giving the Taqdeer Life family an exquisite creation to cherish as their own, Alhamdulillah.

My hope is that you experience Taqdeer as a practical and realistic tool in cultivating an Alhamdulillah mind-set, and that this combined with the remembrance of God, improves your connection with Him (swt). Use this tool to make time for yourself and better yourself holistically, Insha'Allah.

Taqdeer is *More Than Just a Journal.*

Duas,

Samia

CONTENTS

GLOSSARY

ADHKAR	Remembrance of Allah
*ALHAMDULILLAH	Praise be to God For showing gratitude to Allah
BISMILLAH	In the name of God
BISMILLAH HIR RAHMAN HIR RAHEEM	In the name of God, Most Gracious, Most Merciful
*INSHA'ALLAH	God-Willing For expressing a desire to do something
*MASHA'ALLAH	As Allah-Willed For expressing appreciation of something good
NIYYAH	Intention
SHUKR	Gratitude
TAQDEER	Appreciation

Our logo appears as a symbol on every journal page, indicating an entry for the morning and an entry for the evening.

*common phrases of remembrance

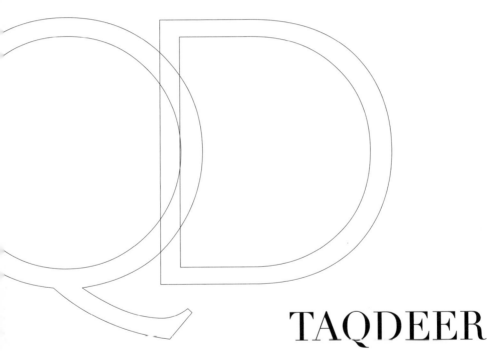

TAQDEER

Our Philosophy | Our Family | Our Brand

Our Philosophy

Taqdeer is an Islamic lifestyle brand that is built on the principles of developing self-improvement, emotional and spiritual well-being. Inspired by creativity and its potential on human development, our unique brand purpose showcases emerging and established artists; all journals come with an artwork postcard designed by an artist. With environmental sustainability in mind, our products are plastic-free and recyclable.

Our Family

This personal touch to our journaling experience is a unique feature to Taqdeer. Using the What Connects You? questions, members of the Taqdeer Life family relay their own personal perspectives when contemplating thankfulness/Shukr. Browse through The Journal section to find our favourite responses.

When do you remember Him (swt)?
How would you define a blessing?
What motivates you to complete your day?
Who are you thankful to?
What do you appreciate about yourself?
Gratitude - What is your why?

Have your own to share?
We would love to know at: salaam@taqdeer.life

Our Brand

INTENTIONS AND NEW BEGINNINGS

The story behind our logo depicts the Sun during the stages of sunrise and sunset thus creating an association between the remembrance of Allah (swt) in the form of Adhkars at these prescribed times. Further as intentions tend to be renewed at the start and end of the day, we felt this connected well with the completion of journal entries both in the morning and evening.

THE JOURNAL COVER

A simple journaling concept is enhanced by a simple cover. We love the feel of a cloth-based cover to evoke a tactile sensory response. We have offered this cover to you as a blank canvas to ornament Taqdeer to your unique and personal taste.

TAQDEER & ART

Promoting Art & Well-being

Promoting Art & Well-being

"Art for me is a form of prayer – I use the verses of Sacred Islamic scripture to remember our human connection with the Eternal."
Maaida Noor

Inspired by creativity and its potential on human development, Taqdeer promotes the arts by supporting emerging and established artists that capture the theme of spirituality in their work. We take this opportunity to showcase artwork kindly created by award winning and international contemporary Islamic artist, Ms. Maaida Noor.

'Jalla Jalalahu'
'May His glory be glorified'

Inspired by the Islamic traditional arts, Islamic illumination forms a detailed floral decoration or 'shamsa' surrounding the sacred words 'Jalla Jalalahu' جَلَّ جَلَالَهُ in addition to the tall Kufic scripted majestic word, 'Allah'.

Jalla Jalalahu encompasses traditional artistic elements. This combined with the use of line and triangular composition creates depth and compliments Taqdeer's logo to elicit a contemporary feel.

MS. MAAIDA NOOR
www.maaidanoor.com | @maaidanoor

WHO, WHAT, WHY & HOW

Who is Taqdeer for? | What makes Taqdeer different?

How will Taqdeer benefit you? | Bulllet Journaling

Why Taqdeer? | How long does it take?

REFLECTION
is the LAMP *of the* HEART.

If it departs, the heart will have *no light.*

IMAM AL-HADDAD

Who is Taqdeer for?

Taqdeer is for those who have never really considered the concept of journaling as well as those who have found the benefits in writing down and reflecting in a journal.

You don't have to be a great writer or feel pressured by the task of writing a vast amount. Taqdeer enables you to build a regular self-reflective gratitude log, one that can be later reflected on, in a manner that is simple yet effective to your positive well-being. Remember the journaling process feels easier to perform once this becomes a consistent habit mastered through practise.

In previous years, scientists found that daily activities accounted for 40 per cent of our happiness[3], Taqdeer encourages closer reflection of your life with strong emphasis on the present so that you can identify and influence your own positive experiences. This is important to leading a happier life and developing an Alhamdulillah mind-set. Over time your journal entries form a record, which can help you to keep track of your development.

Taqdeer offers you a means to make Shukr (gratitude) and remembrance to Allah (swt) the heart of regular focus.

---

[3]*The Greater Good Science Centre at The University of Berkeley (2014) The Science of Happiness.*

"It's not
material success
that determines
whether we have
made it. It's about
whether we are
striving towards a
meaningful way of
life. It's whether we
can be of service in
the lives of others."

SAMIA

What makes Taqdeer different?

Taqdeer is not your cliché gratitude journal. Taqdeer's Alhamdulillah journaling experience is based on research considering the effects of an expressive gratitude strategy in lieu with Islamic principles.

Researchers Ali Youssef Al-Seheel and Noraini M. Noor found that correlating blessings to the remembrance of Allah (swt) increased respondents' levels of happiness due to the connection between beliefs and values. Such an approach can prove to be beneficial for most adult groups.

Through expressing the things that you are appreciative for, Taqdeer also steers your attention towards others you are grateful for in your life and their admirable qualities

Again based on scientific research, the act of doing for others can generate a sentiment of inner gratitude that can lead to increased happiness. For example, writing a letter telling someone why you are grateful to have them in your life or gifting to others can make you feel good about yourself whilst also spreading a little appreciation. The **Task Time** activities found within the journal promotes this notion.

Often we may relate gratitude to counting our blessings and give little thought to how we can use these blessings in a manner that aims to seek Allah's (swt) pleasure. How can we use our blessings for personal growth as well as benefiting others?

What makes Taqdeer truly different to other journals? Throughout the journal are gratitude excerpts relevant to our What Connects You? questions as seen on page 20. This personal touch to our journaling experience is a unique feature as members of the Taqdeer Life family relay their own personal perspectives when contemplating thankfulness/Shukr.

We also feature the work of established and emerging artists.

Lastly, we have not provided an example of a journal entry reflecting a typical day. Remember these entries are personal and unique to you and should not be influenced by anything else.

Taqdeer aims to develop an attitude that cultivates gratitude of the good He (swt) has bestowed within and around us.

How will Taqdeer benefit you?

Improve God consciousness
Cultivate an Alhamdulillah mind-set
Develop psychological mindedness via self-awareness
and introspection habits
Understand the scientific and Islamic benefits of cultivating gratefulness
Nurture spiritual, emotional and psychological health and well-being
Learn al-muraqabah (Islamic mindfulness) practices
Connect blessings of everyday life with the remembrance of Allah (swt)
Refine emotional intelligence through emotion exploration

SELF-RECOGNITION AND VALUES

The 'I appreciate about myself' prompts on the journal entry pages are for you to recognise your gifts, and how you can be in service to others. Not to be confused with arrogance or vanity, positive recognition of the self is encouraged in our faith. This recognition is a process of developing self-awareness of the attributes He (swt) has blessed you with. Identifying and valuing what you are good at nurtures your self-worth and compassion towards self.

The way we view ourselves can influence how we feel about ourselves and vice versa. Self-knowledge of our qualities, strengths and achievements can help us to feel positive about ourselves[4]. When we feel good about ourselves, we are more likely to treat others well as we may cultivate greater values like compassion, generosity and kindness. Thus if seeking to improve our character and behaviour towards others, we need to take a closer look at the strength of our values system, which is very much connected to self-recognition.

"Things begin to happen when we believe in ourselves. For that to happen, we have to remind ourselves daily of our strengths." - Samia

Gratitude isn't just about the utterance of Alhamdulillah. Unlike other gratitude journals, Taqdeer wants you to be specific. Descriptive or detailed accounts about what you are appreciative for can create an effective gratitude recording experience thus increasing happiness.

Our recurring pages titled **Notes, Thoughts & Plans** offers space to jot down contemplations in a little more detail including deeper reflection of the ways in which you can put your blessings to good use.

[4]*Armstrong (2011) U.K. Twelve steps to a compassionate heart*

Gratitude

is not just the utterance of **Alhamdulillah** it's about how you use your blessings to please **Allah** (swt).

Bullet Journaling

As Taqdeer promotes holistic well-being, a bullet journal feature has been applied to our Notes, Thoughts & Plans pages due to its benefits in supporting emotional well-being and mental health.[5]

Bullet journaling by simple definition is a system that can help with keeping track of our life activities. The process of designing grids and/or boxes provides structure to how thoughts can be managed and organised.

The great thing about bullet journaling is that you can design the system to suit your needs and preferences. To-do lists, goal-setting, general lists, doodling, designing quotes and affirmations to simply having a space to vent are just some of the ways a bullet feature can be used.

Where the diary entry pages within Taqdeer offer journaling prompts with a structured layout, the advantages of a bullet journal feature on our Notes, Thoughts & Plans pages encourage you to be free and creative with your space.

[5]*Blurt Team (2018) How bullet journaling can help us manage our mental health.*

Why Taqdeer?

Taqdeer aims to help you identify and relate the positive happenings in your life with the remembrance of Allah (swt), which can nurture a happier you.

As Islam considers gratitude a desired habitual practice, Taqdeer seeks to encourage this notion through correlating life blessings with selected phrases and Adhkar that seek to enhance the remembrance of Allah (swt) at the start and end of each day, every day.

There are three page entries which rotate throughout the journal offering variation. Over time the journaling structure will enable you to channel thoughts in a positive way. Being familiar with what you are expected to regularly reflect on can support you in recognising all that evokes a sense of happiness and appreciation, Insha'Allah.

The format is simple and consistent, the only difference being your perception. It's what you choose to bring to the table.

This journal comprises of Quranic verses with a range of quotes, many stemming from personal experiences to inspire positivity and thankfulness. Though the use of many significant duas are recommended within worship, Taqdeer encourages you to also devise your own to establish a more personal focus that is based on your needs.

"Since Taqdeer encourages morning and evening self-reflective practices, we believe that daily Adhkar corresponding to the morning and evening duas as recommended by our Prophet (pbuh), complement the concept of this journaling experience."

SAMIA

the **MOST BELOVED** of deeds to **ALLAH** (swt) are those that are **MOST CONSISTENT,** *even if it is small.*

THE PROPHET (PBUH)

How long does it take?

Presented as a diary entry, the journal prompts encourage you to record your positive experiences.

Optimising your mind-set for positive reflection can develop a disciplined approach to being mindful over the things that generate happiness in your life.

A key element to most things beneficial is consistency. Consistency to learn and refine develops discipline, which can help you to follow through and achieve results.

Designed to take five minutes to complete at the beginning and end of your day, Taqdeer offers a simple tool for promoting regular reflection, helping you to focus on what matters most through Niyyah (intention) whilst encompassing remembrance, appreciation and positivity.

MORNING / EVENING

Our logo appears as a symbol on every journal page, indicating an entry for the morning and an entry for the evening.

THE AIMS

The Great Eight | The Principles

Links to Research

Values and Happiness

Islamic Mindfulness

Owning Your Emotions

The Great Eight

TAQDEER'S REFLECTIVE AIMS

1   **Relay** gratitude of blessings to Allah (swt)
through a consistent and reflective approach

2   **Remember** Allah (swt) at the start, during,
and end of each day, every day

3   **Improve** self-awareness of
the positives in your life

4   **Focus** on days, events and experiences
from a perspective of gratitude

5   **Contemplate** how you can put
your blessings to good use

6   **Record** current positive happenings that can at
times be easily missed or clouded by challenging
events as well as reflecting on the blessings
arising from these difficult times

7   **Monitor** and establish patterns that have triggered
the act of gratitude for future self-reflection

8   **Develop** what is within your capacity to shape
your future to reach a state of increased
happiness and positive well-being

remember
ME,
I will remember
YOU.

The Principles

Contrary to what you may believe... how we perceive our present can influence our 'happiness'.

Many of us are chasing happiness. Many of us overrate where we expect to attain happiness. Many of us are blessed with success and are fortunate enough to be granted most of what we seek, yet dissatisfaction creeps in and we begin yearning for our next shot of happiness. Valuing our blessings requires a degree of qana'ah (contentment), which is appreciating what we have in comparison to others who are less fortunate.

If we are to truly exercise Tawakkul, trust and reliance in Allah (swt), then we are in some way surrendering to what is beyond our control, we are surrendering to His Will and consequently surrendering to life.

So what if we were to change our mind-set from pursuing happiness to appreciating what we already have? Would that make us happier?

GRATITUDE + PRAISE = ALHAMDULILLAH

Let's be honest - life isn't always wonderful. Life can be pretty difficult at times. A normal day can be a mixture of ups and downs, the good and the bad. Of course there will be situations that are undoubtedly better than others, however the happiness factor can greatly lie with how you perceive situations. Much depends on whether you are able to establish meaning of the present to create those 'Alhamdulillah' moments.

SHUKR JOURNALING = HAPPINESS

Unlike diary writing, journaling is simply a technique to connect your present state with happiness.

When combined with the concept of Shukr (gratitude), all those Alhamdulillah moments become clearer. Even when situations haven't transpired as initially hoped or perceived negative experiences have occurred, identifying and valuing the good in those conditions or simply accepting that circumstance for what it is becomes a process that can foster a more positive perception. This can help towards making you feel happier, particularly if you view the experience as an opportunity for growth.

It is also shaping an awareness that 'Alhamdulillah' seeks to praise and thank Allah (swt) in challenging times, not just the good.

Regarded as an emotional state, gratitude is the ability to express appreciation which promotes resilience and improves personal and relational well-being. The act of genuinely expressing and feeling appreciation of self, others and circumstances through journaling can increase happiness. Similarly identifying how one's own behaviours can relay gratitude to others i.e. praising a colleague's accomplishment, conveying thanks or kindness to someone who has helped you etc can also nurture inner happiness.

Links to Research

Research surrounding positive psychology claims that appreciating all that presently exists, including what your life would be like without those things are key determinants to effective gratitude journaling

Life itself presents many daily challenges. All too often our brains are wired to ruminate and dwell over negative events eventually overshadowing the positives in our lives. Though gratitude can be expressed in many ways, often it is through mental reflection. Psychologists believe that the actual process of documenting develops a greater sense of appreciation. Additionally, documenting can increase levels of self-awareness as personal insights in to yourself can help you to detect and establish both positive and negative patterns in thoughts and behaviours.

Beneficially, experiencing gratitude also triggers a release of dopamine and serotonin in the brain that can enhance happiness. According to research, increased happiness as an outcome of being thankful can help boost your immune system and improve sleep.[6]

Taqdeer wants you to re-wire your brain to focus on the good – consistent practise of this can enhance your state of positive well-being (Insha'Allah).

---

[6] *Y. Barak, The immune system and happiness*

THE KEY TO CONTENTMENT IS TO APPRECIATE WHAT YOU HAVE.

#qana'ah

Values and Happiness

Exercising values and virtues that are important to you help shape positive feelings. A values system that is consistently acted on fosters inner happiness.

Rather than searching for happiness, try to search for meaning and purpose that are in line with your values. When you do this, happiness occurs more often.

At the beginning of each week (or month), select a value to develop and document the acts you carried out to achieve your chosen value. Recording enables you to measure your commitment in achieving the value and also helps you to identify what may require developing. Aim to carry out your chosen value three or four times a week.

GENEROSITY
example, I offered my skills to help voluntarily.
HUMILITY
example, I took on feedback, even though it was hard.
PATIENCE
example, I listened, properly, and didn't interrupt.
KINDNESS
example, I left some food at their usual spot.
SERVICE
example, I am using my knowledge to spread the message of healing.
GRATITUDE
example, I will thank my supervisor for her honesty.
FORGIVENESS
example, I forgave myself for...

When materialistic desires harbour within the heart, and not in the hands, unhealthy attachments can form. This can affect both our spiritual and psychological well-being. Throughout the course of our lives we will make choices that determine how we live and the quality of life we wish to lead. The majority of those choices will reflect our values system. Cultivating a values system that encourages service and purpose has the potential to increase happiness. Importantly, when we make an active effort to practise the virtue of gratitude, we are also cultivating important values like humility and generosity, which can support our well-being.

Wealth,
authority
and
power
do not change a man,
they only

REVEAL

HIM.

ALI IBN ABU TALIB (AS)

Islamic Mindfulness

Within the Islamic context, silence is related to the virtue muraqabah, denoting 'presence' in Arabic[7]. Our daily prayers and quiet reflective worship are times when we cultivate muraqabah.

Extending this further, we can connect this with Islamic mindfulness otherwise known as 'Al-muraqabah', which is a meditative spiritual state that consciously engages our mind, heart and awareness to Allah (swt).[8]

Within our journal page entries, you will notice 'Islamic mindfulness focus' encouraging you to make a conscious effort to allocate days within each month to cultivate Al-muraqabah.

Similar to most mindfulness meditative exercises, it is essential that you find a quiet time in the day to nurture Al-muraqabah practice preferably in the morning. Pay close attention to your breathing, thoughts and awareness of Allah (swt). It's normal for your thoughts to drift, the skill is observing when this happens and bringing your attention back to Al-muraqabah. This also helps to strengthen awareness of your 'observer' thoughts. Begin with one-three minutes per session and extend this time as you become more consistent and comfortable with practise.

[7] *Quddus, S. (2020) Trust in Allah, but tie your camel.*
[8] *Parrott, J. (2017) How to be a mindful Muslim: an exercise in Islamic meditation.*

OUR ISLAMIC MINDFULNESS FOCUS IS SIMPLE

Reflect in mind and heart thanking Allah (swt) for all your blessings and all that He (swt) has given you.

Acknowledge the presence of angels witnessing your silent meditation and their prayers upon you for remembering Allah (swt).[9]

Focus thoughts on the time you have made to remember Allah (swt) and thank Him for enabling the opportunity to reflect.

Exercise through fully engaged dhikr 'Alhamdulillah' (praise and gratitude) for Allah (swt) beginning with 100 times.

Exercise through fully engaged dhikr 'Subhaan Allahi wa bi hamdihi' (Glory and praise to Allah (swt) beginning with 100 times, extend this with practise.

Contemplate how you can improve future Al-muraqabah practice for example, utilise time after fajr prayers, limit anything that distracts your attention etc.

Identify opportunities to demonstrate thanks to Allah (swt) by carrying out pleasing, righteous deeds.

Choose and learn the meaning of Allah's (swt) name that aligns with a value from your values list. Perform invocation and dhikr using His (swt) name with mindful attention to its meaning and significance in your life. Continue this process, selecting a different name as you cover a new value. Can you do this with all His (swt) 99 names, Insha'Allah?

[9] Al-Ashkar, U.S. (2003) The World of The Noble Angels.

If you could hear the
SOUND
of the PENS
of the angels writing your name
among those who remember
ALLAH
(swt), you would be
bewildered out of joy.

IBN QAYYIM AL-JAWZIYYA

Owning Your Emotions

Generally labelling emotions whether positive or negative nurtures self-awareness of your mood in the present moment. Cultivating self-awareness is consistent with Islamic psychology and key to leading an Islamic-adherent lifestyle. This includes practising and developing self-reflection and introspection.[10]

Validating not so good emotional states and processing these emotions is just as important as acknowledging positive feelings. Key to emotional health and developing resilience is validating the thoughts and feelings we try to avoid. This acknowledgement facilitates a 'containing' state as highlighted in psychotherapeutic theory.[11] Though Taqdeer's main theme is to support the practice of thinking positively, you are also encouraged to confront and reflect on those difficult emotions.

Emotional resilience is developed by acknowledging all felt-states. Accept what you feel, validate and seek strength in Alhamdulillah.

[10]*Keshavarzi and Haque, (2013) Outlining a Psychotherapy Model for Enhancing Muslim Mental Health within and Islamic Context*
[11]*Bion, W. (1970) Container and Contained: Attention and Interpretation.*

ALL EMOTIONS WERE

created
by *Him* (SWT)

FACT #1

Psychologists using functional Magnetic Resonance Imaging (fMRI) when examining human emotions found that in situations where negative emotions were felt, using one or two words to name those feelings minimilised their effect leading to better emotional responses.

FACT #2

Professor of psychology, Matthew D. Lieberman states that negative emotions can increase activity in the part of the brain called the amygdala, influencing how we respond. If these emotions are labelled, another part of the brain within the right ventrolateral prefrontal cortex of the brain results in increased activity that can lead to the processing of these emotions hence, fostering constructive responses.

FACT #3

An expert in social psychology, Professor James Pennebaker claims that suppressing uncomfortable feelings and the inability to discuss these emotions can affect levels of immune functioning in men. The concept of journaling has been found to be beneficial in providing males with privacy and a safe space to record thoughts and express feelings hence, fostering an 'offloading' process.

FACT #4

The part of the brain that forms decisions is also the part of the brain where emotions originate.

FACT #5

Acknowledging how you are feeling can help you to reflect on how you are going to deal with those emotions, particularly negative ones. Practicing this form of mindfulness by naming those feelings in a few words or sentences can benefit your overall mood and state of positivity. Very simply…

CURB THE EMOTION BY NAMING IT.[12]

12 *"Name it to tame it"* - *Professor Dr Dan J. Siegel*

MY NIYYAH

Connect the Dots | Steps to Success | My Niyyah

Connect the Dots

Take some time to think about the words on these pages. Try to be specific as you write all that comes to mind. Below are a few prompts to begin with:

What's my definition?
When do I feel this the most?
Where am I right now?
Where would I like to be?
Examples in my life?

HAPPINESS

GRATITUDE

ALLAH (swt)

Definitely
all ACTIONS
are (based) on
INTENTIONS.

SAHIH BUKHARI

Steps to Success

Taqdeer is about developing manageable empowering habits. Successful consistency in application is about you learning and cultivating these habits.

The key to anything beneficial is consistency and involves making a long-term commitment. Commitment to change resulting in positive well-being requires effort. Effort, to be effective, necessitates renewing Niyyah (intention) to be in the present moment when focusing on the positive happenings of your day to express gratitude successfully.

Some scientists claim that on average, the least amount of time that it takes to form new habits is 21 days. Therefore, consistency and commitment are paramount to achieving regularity.

THE MAIN INTENTION IS...

For any journaling technique to be effective and achieve the results desired, a necessary prerequisite is the intention to be motivated in order to experience increased happiness[13]. The benefits of journaling to cultivate an Alhamdulillah mind-set is that it can help you to focus on the good and the blessings in your life. This alleviates comparisons with others, which in turn improves your relationship with Allah (swt).

Wholeheartedly making these aspects as part of your intention to journal will make your journaling experience effective and support both your spiritual as well as emotional health.

[13] *Psychologist Sonja Lyubomirsky*

Interestingly, how much gratitude a person feels in a certain situation is believed to be dependent on a number of cognitive factors. This means that Niyyah (intention) is even more vital, especially when in a benefactor position. Are intentions serving altruism/ altruistic wishes, or rather self-serving needs, such as wishing to improve one's reputation.[14]

Reminding ourselves that everything we do for the sake of Allah (swt), for His blessings, is key to ensuring that our intention remains aligned with God's (swt) pleasure. Continuously reflecting on our Niyyah is an effective way to improve our relationship with Allah (swt).

[14]The Greater Good Science Centre at The University of Berkeley (2018) The Science of Gratitude

Therefore,

I MAKE NIYYAH TO...

Be *motivated* to experience increased happiness (Insha'Allah).   Y / N

Cultivate an Alhamdulillah mind-set (Insha'Allah).   Y / N

Improve my *relationship* with Allah (swt) (Insha'Allah).   Y / N

ACHIEVED BY...

Documenting *Taqdeer* (appreciation) through
the remembrance of Allah (swt) as a regular habit.   Y / N

Completing the *morning and evening* sections
of a journal page at their intended times.   Y / N

Spending *five minutes* to journal, every other day.   Y / N

MY NIYYAH

SEIZE
IT WITH
INSHA'
ALLAH

ADHKAR

Remembrance of Allah

Morning and Evening

The
FRUITS of
DHIKR

Dhikr of the heart
and tongue leads one to
know Allah (swt), inspires
love, encourages *modesty,*
and leads to fear and
self-examination.
It *keeps one* from falling
short in *obedience* to Him
and *prevents* one from
taking sins lightly.

IBN AL-QAYYIM

Remembrance of Allah (swt)

There are many Adhkar of the morning and the evening[15] corresponding to the beginning and ending of the day. Considered to be at the heart of worship, their habitual practice can contribute towards a state of positive well-being and happiness.

Morning Adhkar
Between Fajr and Sunrise

Evening Adhkar
Between Asr and Maghrib

PHRASES OF REMEMBRANCE

Alhamdulillah
Praise be to God | For showing gratitude to Allah (swt)

Insha'Allah
God-Willing | For expressing a desire to do something

Masha'Allah
As Allah-Willed | For expressing appreciation of something good

---

[15] *Al-Qahtani, Saudi Arabia. Fortification of the Muslim through remembrance and supplication from the Qur'aan and Sunnah.*

Morning and Evening

Asbahnaa wa 'asbahal-mulku [Amsaynaa wa'amsal-mulku] lillahi walhamdul lillahi, laa 'ilahaa 'illallahu wahdahu laa shareeka lahu, lahul mulku wa lahul-hamdu wa Huwa alaa kulli shay'in Qadeer. Rabbi 'as 'aluka khayra maa fee hathal-yawmi [hathihil-laylati] wa sharri maa ba'dahu [ba'dahaa], Rabbi 'a'oothu bika minal-kasali, wa soo 'il-kibari, Rabbi 'a'oothu bika min 'athaabin fin-naari wa 'athaabin fil-qabri.

We have reached the morning/evening and at this very time unto Allah belongs all sovereignty, and all praise is for Allah. None has the right to be worshipped except Allah, alone, without partner, to Him belongs all sovereignty and praise and He is over all things omnipotent.

My Lord, I ask You for the good of this day (night) and the good of what follows it and I take refuge in You from the evil of this day/night and the evil of what follows it. My Lord, I take refuge in You from laziness and senility. My Lord, I take refuge in You from torment in the fire and punishment in the grave.

Allahumma bika 'asbahnaa, wa bika 'amsaynaa wa bika nahyaa, wa bika namootu wa 'ilaykan-nushoor.

O Allah, by your leave we have reached the morning and by Your leave we have reached the evening, by Your leave we live and die and unto You is our resurrection.

*Allahumma bika 'amsaynaa, wa bika asbahnaa wa bika nahyaa,
wa bika namoot wa 'ilaykal-maseer*

O Allah, by Your leave we have reached the evening and by Your
leave we have reached the morning, by Your leave we live and die
and unto You is our return.

*Allahumma 'innee 'asbahtu [amsaytu] 'ush-hiduka wa 'ush-hidu
hamalata 'arshika, wa malaa'ikataka wajamee'a khalqika, 'annaka
'Antallaahu laa ilaaha 'illaa 'Anta wahdaka laa shareeka laka wa 'anna
Mummadan 'abduka wa Rasooluka.*
(Four times in the morning and evening)

O Allah, verily I have reached the morning [evening] and call on
You, the bearers of Your throne, Your angels, and all of Your creation
to witness that You are Allah, none has the right to be worshipped
except You, alone, without partner and that Muhammad (peace and
blessings be upon him) is Your Servant and Messenger.

SAYYIDAL ISTIGHFAR
THE CHIEF OF PRAYERS FOR FORGIVENESS

*Allahumma 'Anta Rabbee, la 'ilaaha 'illaa 'Anta khalaqtanee wa anaa
'abduka, wa 'anaa 'alaa 'ahdika wa wa'dika mas-tata'tu 'a 'oothu bika
min sharri maa sana'tu aboo'u laka bi-ni' matika 'alayya, wa 'aboo 'u
bithanbee faghfir lee fa 'innahu la yaghfiru thunooba illa 'Anta.*

O Allah, You are my Lord, none has the right to be worshipped
except You, You created me and I am Your servant and I abide to
Your covenant and promise as best I can, I take refuge in You from
the evil of which I have committed. I acknowledge Your favour upon
me and I acknowledge my sin, so forgive me, for verily none can
forgive sin except You.

Astaghfiruka w' atuboo ilayk

I seek Your forgiveness, Allah, and repent unto You.

Verily,
in the
remembrance of Allah (swt)
do
HEARTS find
REST.

DUA FOR HEALTH AND WELL-BEING OF FACULTIES

Allahumma 'aafinee fee badanee, Allahumma 'aafinee fee sam'ee,
Allahumma 'aafinee fee basaree, laa 'ilaaha 'illaa Anta.
Three times

O Allah, grant my body health, O Allah, grant my hearing health,
O Allah, grant my sight health. None has the right to be
worshipped except You.

Allahumma 'innee 'a'oothu bika minal-kufri, walfaqri, wa 'a'oothu bika
min 'athaabil-qabri, laa 'ilaaha 'ilaa Anta.
Three times

O Allah, I take refuge with You from disbelief and poverty, and I take
refuge with You from the punishment of the grave; none has the
right to be worshipped except You.

DUA TO OFFER THANKS

Allâhumma maa 'asbaha bee (if evening: Allahumma maa 'amsaa bee) min ni'matin 'aw bi'ahadin min khalqika, faminka wahdaka laa shareeka laka. falakal-hamdu wa lakash-shukru.

O Allah, what blessing I or any of Your creation have risen upon, is from You alone, without partner, so for You is all praise and unto You all thanks.

DUA FOR RELIANCE ON ALLAH (SWT)

Hasbiyallaahu laa ilaaha 'illa Huwa 'alayhi tawakkaltu, wa Huwa Rabbu-l-'Arshil-Adheem.
Seven times in the morning and evening

Allah is Sufficient for me, none has the right to be worshipped except Him, upon Him I rely and He is Lord of the exalted throne.

And whatever of

BLESSINGS

&

GOOD
THINGS

you have,
it is from Allah (swt).

DUA FOR PARDON, PROTECTION AND WELL-BEING

*Allaahumma 'innee 'as'alukal-'afwa wal'aafiyata fid-dunyaa
wal'aakhirati, Allaahumma 'innee 'as'alukal-'afwa wal'aafiyata
fee deenee wa dunyaaya wa 'ahlee, wa maalee, Allaahum-mastur
'awraatee, wa 'aamin raw'aatee, Allaahum-mahfadhnee min bayni
yadayya, wa min khalfee, wa 'an yameenee, wa 'an shimaalee, wa min
fawqee, wa 'a'oothu bi'adhamatika 'an 'ughtaala min tahtee.*

O Allah, I ask You for pardon and well-being in this life and the
next. O Allah, I ask You for pardon and well-being in my religious
and worldly affairs, and my family and my wealth. O Allah, veil my
weaknesses and set at ease my dismay. O Allah, preserve me from
the front and from behind and on my right and on my left and
from above, and I take refuge with You lest I be swallowed up by
the earth.

*Asbahnaa wa 'asbaha [In the evening: Amsaynaa wa amsaa] al-mulku
lillaahi Rabbil-'aalameen, Allaahumma 'innee 'as'aluka khayra haathal-
yawmi [In the evening: haathihil-laylati] Fathahu wa nasrahu wa
noorahu, wa barakatahu, wa hudaahu, wa'a'oothu bika min sharri maa
feehi wa sharri maa ba'dahu.*

We have reached the morning/evening and at this very time all
sovereignty belongs to Allah, Lord of the worlds. O Allah, I ask you
of the good of this day/night, its triumphs and its victories, its light
and its blessings and its guidance, and I take refuge in You from the
evil of this day/night and the evil that follows it.

Allaahumma 'Aalimal-ghaybi wash-shahaadati faatiras-samaawaati wal'ardhi, Rabba kulli shay 'in wa maleekahu, 'ash-hadu 'an laa 'ilaaha'illaa 'Anta, 'a'oothu bika min sharri nafsee, wa min sharrish-shaytaani wa shirkihi, wa 'an 'aqtarifa 'alaa nafsee soo'an, 'aw 'ajurrahu'ilaa Muslimin.

O Allah, Knower of the unseen and the seen, Creator of the heavens and the Earth, Lord and Sovereign of all things, I bear witness that none has the right to be worshipped except You. I take refuge in You from the evil of my soul and from the evil and shirk of the devil, and from committing wrong against my soul or bringing such upon another Muslim.

DUA TO STAY ON THE PATH OF ISLAM

Asbahnaa 'alaa fitratil-'Islaami [In the evening: Amsaynaa 'alaa fitratil-'Islaam] wa 'alaa kalimatil-'ikhlaasi, wa 'alaa deeni Nabiyyinaa Muhammadin (sallallaahu 'alayhi wa sallama), wa 'alaa millati 'abeenaa 'Ibraaheema, haneefan Musliman wa maa kaana minal-mushrikeen.

We rise upon the fitrah (i.e. the religion of Islam, the way of Ibrahim saw) of Islam, and the word of pure faith (the Shahaadah), and upon the religion of our Prophet Muhammad (peace & blessings be upon him) and the religion of our forefather Ibrahim, who was a Muslim and of true faith and was not of those who associate others with Allah.

DUA TO AVOID SUDDEN AFFLICTIONS

Bismillaahil-lathee laa yadhurru ma'as-mihi shay'un fil-'ardhi wa laa fis-samaa'i wa Huwas-Samee 'ul- 'Aleem.
Three times

In the name of Allah with whose name nothing is harmed on earth nor in the heavens and He is The All-Seeing, The All-Knowing.

DUA FOR SUPPORT AND ASSISTANCE

Yaa Hayyu yaa Qayyoomu birahmatika 'astagheethu 'aslih lee sha'nee kullahu wa laa takilnee 'ilaa nafsee tarfata 'aynin.

O Ever Living, O Self-Subsisting and Supporter of all, by Your mercy I seek assistance, rectify for me all of my affairs and do not leave me to myself, even for the blink of an eye.

DUA FOR AFFIRMATION OF FAITH

Radheetu billaahi Rabban, wa bil-'Islaami deenan, wa bi-Muhammadin (sallallaahu 'alayhi wa sallama) Nabiyyan.
Three times

I am pleased with Allah as a Lord, and Islam as a religion and Muhammad (peace and blessings be upon him) as a Prophet.

DUA TO PRAISE ALLAH (SWT)

Laa ilaaha illa l-laahu wahdahu laa sharîka lah(u) lahu-l-mulku walahu-l-hamd(u), wa Huwa alaa kulli shay'in Qadeer.
Once or one hundred times everyday

None has the right to be worshipped except Allah, alone, without partner, to Him belongs all sovereignty and praise, and He is over all things omnipotent.

DUA TO RELAY IMMEASURABLE PRAISE TO ALLAH (SWT)

Subhanal-lahi wabihamdih, 'adada khalqihi warida nafsih, wazinata 'arshih, wamidada kalimatih.
Three times

How perfect Allah is and I praise Him by the number of His creation and His pleasure, and by the weight of His throne, and the ink of His words.

DUA FOR BLESSINGS

*Allahumma inni 'as'aluka 'ilman naafi'an, wa rizqan tayyiban,
wa 'amalan mutaqabbalan.*
To be said after giving Saalam for the Fajr prayer

O Allah, I ask You for knowledge which is beneficial and sustenance
which is good, and deeds which are acceptable.

SALAWAT UPON THE PROPHET (PBUH)

Allahumma salli wa sallim alaa nabiyyinaa Muhammadin
Ten times

O Allah, send prayers and blessings upon our prophet Muhammad
(peace and blessings be upon him)

DUA FOR PROTECTION

Aoothu bi-kalimati l-laahi-t-taammaati min sharri maa khalaq
Three times in the evening

I take refuge in Allah's perfect words from the evil He has created.

DUA TO CONVEY GRATITUDE

Allahumma a'inni ala dhikrika, wa shukrika wa husni 'ibadatika.

O Allah, help me remember You, to be grateful to You,
and to worship You in an excellent manner. (Abu Dawud)

GRATIFYING ALLAH'S (SWT) PERFECTION

Subhaanallaahi wa bihamdihi.
One hundred times

How perfect Allah is and I praise Him.

BISMILLAH

MORNING

I am feeling...

My chosen value and how I will act upon it this week...

EVENING

Three Alhamdulillah moments...

What matters today and/or the next few days...

I appreciate about myself...

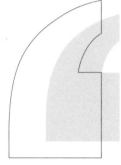

Who are you thankful to?

Anyone who contributes in bettering my life. Those who are honest with you. Those who wish to see you do well. Those who don't judge you. Ultimately I'm thankful to God for His continued blessings.

FARRAH AZAM, UK

MORNING

I am feeling...

Islamic Mindfulness: I will practise Al-muraqabah this week on these days and times....

EVENING

Three Alhamdulillah moments...

Masha'Allah I admire (who, what and why)...

I am grateful (to, for, to have)...

I see
and speak
of the beauty
I see within
others.

MORNING

I am feeling...

Insha'Allah I will make the next few days great by...

EVENING

Three Alhamdulillah moments...

Three things that made me smile the past few days...

I acted on my chosen value this week by....

MORNING

I am feeling...

My chosen value and how I will act upon it this week...

EVENING

Three Alhamdulillah moments...

What matters today and/or the next few days...

I appreciate about myself...

{*task* time}

BUY SOMEONE A LITTLE GIFT.

The Prophet (pbuh) used to accept gifts and reward people for giving them.
Al-Bukhari

Every time you buy someone a gift, they receive the blessing but you receive the reward. That's because gifting increases your love for one another and is an act of selflessness that is beloved.

MORNING

I am feeling...

Islamic Mindfulness: I will practise Al-muraqabah this week on these days and times....

EVENING

Three Alhamdulillah moments...

Masha'Allah I admire (who, what and why)...

I am grateful (to, for, to have)...

He who
does not
THANK
PEOPLE,
does not
THANK
ALLAH
(swt)

ABU HURAIRAH (RA)

MORNING

I am feeling...

Insha'Allah I will make the next few days great by...

EVENING

Three Alhamdulillah moments...

Three things that made me smile the past few days...

I acted on my chosen value this week by....

MORNING

I am feeling...

My chosen value and how I will act upon it this week...

EVENING

Three Alhamdulillah moments...

What matters today and/or the next few days...

I appreciate about myself...

"I forgave, because He
(swt) is Just. I forgave,
because it's for my
sake. I forgave, so that
He (swt) forgives me.
I forgave, because
ultimately, this energy
is best spent on me.

People may hurt you,
life events may test you,
but you are responsible
for your emotional
healing. Choose you."

SAMIA

MORNING

I am feeling...

Islamic Mindfulness: I will practise Al-muraqabah this week on these days and times....

EVENING

Three Alhamdulillah moments...

Masha'Allah I admire (who, what and why)...

I am grateful (to, for, to have)...

YOU

CHOOSE

TO

SEEK

THE

SILVER

LINING

MORNING

I am feeling...

Insha'Allah I will make the next few days great by...

EVENING

Three Alhamdulillah moments...

Three things that made me smile the past few days...

I acted on my chosen value this week by....

MORNING

I am feeling...

My chosen value and how I will act upon it this week...

EVENING

Three Alhamdulillah moments...

What matters today and/or the next few days...

I appreciate about myself...

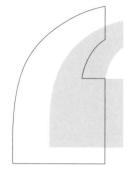

Gratitude.
What is
your why?

Because Allah said so. Because it can make things better – and if not better than at least not worse. Because people are all Allah's creation and deserve to be treated the way that I would want to be treated myself. Because I don't know a lot in the scheme of things. Because I want things to be beautiful and blessed in every aspect of my life and the lives of others around me. Why not? Let's see what happens. Because happiness and fun is not a crime. Because I don't want to be that person in the future. Because we have an amazing history as Muslims and I don't want to be the person that dishonours that.

RUMANA KABIR, UK

MORNING

I am feeling...

Islamic Mindfulness: I will practise Al-muraqabah this week on these days and times....

EVENING

Three Alhamdulillah moments...

Masha'Allah I admire (who, what and why)...

I am grateful (to, for, to have)...

Know that *thankfulness* is from the
HIGHEST of STATIONS,
and it is *higher than* patience and fear and detachment of the
WORLD.

IMAM AL-GHAZALI

MORNING

I am feeling...

Insha'Allah I will make the next few days great by...

EVENING

Three Alhamdulillah moments...

Three things that made me smile the past few days...

I acted on my chosen value this week by....

MORNING

I am feeling...

My chosen value and how I will act upon it this week...

EVENING

Three Alhamdulillah moments...

What matters today and/or the next few days...

I appreciate about myself...

{task time}

SEND SOMEONE A THANK YOU MESSAGE

(and try to do this daily Insha'Allah). Giving thanks (tashakkur) to others for their favours and kindness is encouraged in our faith.

MORNING

I am feeling...

Islamic Mindfulness: I will practise Al-muraqabah this week on these days and times....

EVENING

Three Alhamdulillah moments...

Masha'Allah I admire (who, what and why)...

I am grateful (to, for, to have)...

AllahTawakkul

MORNING

I am feeling...

Insha'Allah I will make the next few days great by...

EVENING

Three Alhamdulillah moments...

Three things that made me smile the past few days...

I acted on my chosen value this week by....

MORNING

I am feeling...

My chosen value and how I will act upon it this week...

EVENING

Three Alhamdulillah moments...

What matters today and/or the next few days...

I appreciate about myself...

"Be true to yourself. In a bid to be falsely liked, disconnecting from who we really are can deeply impact our sense of self. It's a difficult world out there so lead your life with authenticity that reflects values which are true to you.

And remember, authenticity also requires working on those 'shadow' traits; the aspects of ourselves that we wish to unacknowledge and also hide from others."

SAMIA

MORNING

I am feeling...

Islamic Mindfulness: I will practise Al-muraqabah this week on these days and times....

EVENING

Three Alhamdulillah moments...

Masha'Allah I admire (who, what and why)...

I am grateful (to, for, to have)...

Imaan is of *two halves;*
half is
patience
SABR,
and half is being
thankful
SHUKR.

IBN QAYYIM AL-JAWZIYYA

MORNING

I am feeling...

Insha'Allah I will make the next few days great by...

EVENING

Three Alhamdulillah moments...

Three things that made me smile the past few days...

I acted on my chosen value this week by....

MORNING

I am feeling...

My chosen value and how I will act upon it this week...

EVENING

Three Alhamdulillah moments...

What matters today and/or the next few days...

I appreciate about myself...

When do you remember Him (swt)?

I see Him when I travel and observe nature in its raw beauty. I see Him in the work of the bees, the rings around a 200-year-old tree and the formation of rock faces at 3000ft. It makes me remember how small we are in the grand scheme of things and that we are merely drops of ink on His majestic celestial canvas.

ROBI CHOWDHURY, UK

MORNING

I am feeling...

Islamic Mindfulness: I will practise Al-muraqabah this week on these days and times....

EVENING

Three Alhamdulillah moments...

Masha'Allah I admire (who, what and why)...

I am grateful (to, for, to have)...

PRECIOUS YOU ARE HIS (SWT) GIFT TO OTHERS.

MORNING

I am feeling...

Insha'Allah I will make the next few days great by...

EVENING

Three Alhamdulillah moments...

Three things that made me smile the past few days...

I acted on my chosen value this week by....

MORNING

I am feeling...

My chosen value and how I will act upon it this week...

EVENING

Three Alhamdulillah moments...

What matters today and/or the next few days...

I appreciate about myself...

{*task* time}

WHO ARE THEY?

Make a list of all the people in your life whom you are grateful to have. (You will need this list for the final Task Time activity in the Reflection section of the journal).

"The souls are (like) an army joined (in the world of spirits) whichever souls knew each other (in that world) are attracted towards each other (in this world) and whichever remained distant and indifferent (there) are disinterested to each other (in this world)." – The Prophet (pbuh)

MORNING

I am feeling...

Islamic Mindfulness: I will practise Al-muraqabah this week on these days and times....

EVENING

Three Alhamdulillah moments...

Masha'Allah I admire (who, what and why)...

I am grateful (to, for, to have)...

You presume
you are a small entity,
but
WITHIN YOU
is *enfolded*
the
ENTIRE
UNIVERSE.

IMAM ALI (AS)

MORNING

I am feeling...

Insha'Allah I will make the next few days great by...

EVENING

Three Alhamdulillah moments...

Three things that made me smile the past few days...

I acted on my chosen value this week by....

MORNING

I am feeling...

My chosen value and how I will act upon it this week...

EVENING

Three Alhamdulillah moments...

What matters today and/or the next few days...

I appreciate about myself...

"Your worth and your value are not determined by how others treat you. Likewise, the events in your life do not define you. Strive to move forward in life with an approving mind-set and see where it takes you."

SAMIA

MORNING

I am feeling...

Islamic Mindfulness: I will practise Al-muraqabah this week on these days and times....

EVENING

Three Alhamdulillah moments...

Masha'Allah I admire (who, what and why)...

I am grateful (to, for, to have)...

OUR DEEDS
OUR WORK
DEFINE
OUR LEGACY.

MORNING

I am feeling...

Insha'Allah I will make the next few days great by...

EVENING

Three Alhamdulillah moments...

Three things that made me smile the past few days...

I acted on my chosen value this week by....

MORNING

I am feeling...

My chosen value and how I will act upon it this week...

EVENING

Three Alhamdulillah moments...

What matters today and/or the next few days...

I appreciate about myself...

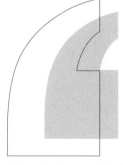

*How would
you define
a blessing?*

A blessing is something that we don't know how we
deserved, that we don't know if we really deserved,
but that gives us hope in the
fact that maybe we did
something good at
some point.

S.F., FRANCE

MORNING

I am feeling...

Islamic Mindfulness: I will practise Al-muraqabah this week on these days and times....

EVENING

Three Alhamdulillah moments...

Masha'Allah I admire (who, what and why)...

I am grateful (to, for, to have)...

And who is
GRATEFUL,
does so to the
PROFIT of his
OWN SOUL.

SURAH LUQMAN | 12

MORNING

I am feeling...

Insha'Allah I will make the next few days great by...

EVENING

Three Alhamdulillah moments...

Three things that made me smile the past few days...

I acted on my chosen value this week by....

MORNING

I am feeling...

My chosen value and how I will act upon it this week...

EVENING

Three Alhamdulillah moments...

What matters today and/or the next few days...

I appreciate about myself...

{task time}

DO SOMETHING THOUGHTFUL FOR SOMEONE

who would appreciate your gesture.
"Every act of kindness is Sadaqah."
The Prophet (pbuh)

MORNING

I am feeling...

Islamic Mindfulness: I will practise Al-muraqabah this week on these days and times....

EVENING

Three Alhamdulillah moments...

Masha'Allah I admire (who, what and why)...

I am grateful (to, for, to have)...

But first, be kind.

MORNING

I am feeling...

Insha'Allah I will make the next few days great by...

EVENING

Three Alhamdulillah moments...

Three things that made me smile the past few days...

I acted on my chosen value this week by....

MORNING

I am feeling...

My chosen value and how I will act upon it this week...

EVENING

Three Alhamdulillah moments...

What matters today and/or the next few days...

I appreciate about myself...

"Strength comes from validating and owning your emotions. It's strength because it's not avoidance and will lead to inner growth, resilience and healing.

Disallowing yourself to feel pent up emotions is unhealthy. Remember, you are not being ungrateful for feeling."

SAMIA

MORNING

I am feeling...

Islamic Mindfulness: I will practise Al-muraqabah this week on these days and times....

EVENING

Three Alhamdulillah moments...

Masha'Allah I admire (who, what and why)...

I am grateful (to, for, to have)...

If we had *perfect power*
to determine our destinies;
and *perfect vision* to see the future
and know what is best for us,
we would choose

EXACTLY THE FATE that ALLAH (swt) has CHOSEN

for us.

IMAM AL-GHAZALI

MORNING

I am feeling...

Insha'Allah I will make the next few days great by...

EVENING

Three Alhamdulillah moments...

Three things that made me smile the past few days...

I acted on my chosen value this week by....

MORNING

I am feeling...

My chosen value and how I will act upon it this week...

EVENING

Three Alhamdulillah moments...

What matters today and/or the next few days...

I appreciate about myself...

When do you remember Him (swt)?

"I remember Him (swt) almost all the time. Especially, I remember Him (swt) when I have second thoughts about a thing, or a deed or an act. When I am blessed with more than I expected. Of course when I am hurt or depressed or when I fear something. I grew up telling myself 'Allah (swt) loves me.' I truly believe He (swt) does. Allah (swt) loves us 70 times more than a mother, as per the hadith. So, it matters to me that I don't do a thing that is disliked by Him (swt) which will distant me from Him (swt). So, I cross check my intentions that I am not disobeying Him(swt). And When I start something new or achieve a goal or fail at something I remember Him (swt) as He (swt) is the best of planners who also loves me and knows what's better for me, who won't ever do anything unjust to me, and trust His (swt) plans. Also, when I start caring a little too much about what people think of/about me, I just disconnect with everyone to spent sometime in His (swt) remembrance thinking I belong to Him (swt) and I shall return to Him (swt) and the world is temporary so it shouldn't bother me."

N.S., UK

MORNING

I am feeling...

Islamic Mindfulness: I will practise Al-muraqabah this week on these days and times....

EVENING

Three Alhamdulillah moments...

Masha'Allah I admire (who, what and why)...

I am grateful (to, for, to have)...

HAPPINESS IS CULTIVATED FROM WITHIN

MORNING

I am feeling...

Insha'Allah I will make the next few days great by...

EVENING

Three Alhamdulillah moments...

Three things that made me smile the past few days...

I acted on my chosen value this week by....

NOTES, THOUGHTS & PLANS

MORNING

I am feeling...

My chosen value and how I will act upon it this week...

EVENING

Three Alhamdulillah moments...

What matters today and/or the next few days...

I appreciate about myself...

{*task* time}

COMPLIMENT SOMEONE

by telling them a quality of theirs that you admire,
and find someone new every month, Insha'Allah.

MORNING

I am feeling...

Islamic Mindfulness: I will practise Al-muraqabah this week on these days and times....

EVENING

Three Alhamdulillah moments...

Masha'Allah I admire (who, what and why)...

I am grateful (to, for, to have)...

Blessings are *connected* to GRATITUDE, and gratitude *leads to more* BLESSINGS, they are attracted to one another.

ALI IBN ABI TALIB

MORNING

I am feeling...

Insha'Allah I will make the next few days great by...

EVENING

Three Alhamdulillah moments...

Three things that made me smile the past few days...

I acted on my chosen value this week by....

NOTES, THOUGHTS & PLANS

MORNING

I am feeling...

My chosen value and how I will act upon it this week...

EVENING

Three Alhamdulillah moments...

What matters today and/or the next few days...

I appreciate about myself...

"Perfection is for machines.
Doing your best for humans.
There is no harm in perfecting
a skill, but this is different. This
is when we seek perfection
in self and others, even the
perceived idealistic life. In an
age where standards continue to
rise, adopting a 'good-enough'
perspective can shift our thinking
towards a glass half full approach.

I will continue to do my best, but
good-enough is where it starts
and ends. What about you?"

SAMIA

MORNING

I am feeling...

Islamic Mindfulness: I will practise Al-muraqabah this week on these days and times....

EVENING

Three Alhamdulillah moments...

Masha'Allah I admire (who, what and why)...

I am grateful (to, for, to have)...

To fall is to rise.

MORNING

I am feeling...

Insha'Allah I will make the next few days great by...

EVENING

Three Alhamdulillah moments...

Three things that made me smile the past few days...

I acted on my chosen value this week by....

MORNING

I am feeling...

My chosen value and how I will act upon it this week...

EVENING

Three Alhamdulillah moments...

What matters today and/or the next few days...

I appreciate about myself...

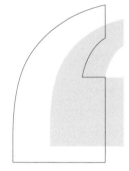

*How would
you define
a blessing?*

When I think of a blessing I try to remember
the little things we take for granted in our every
day lives - food, shelter, rain, nature. Being able to
witness a random act of kindness from someone is
a blessing, if you're reminded
of humanity and how
important it is to be a
good person in your
every day life.

S.F., UK

MORNING

I am feeling...

Islamic Mindfulness: I will practise Al-muraqabah this week on these days and times....

EVENING

Three Alhamdulillah moments...

Masha'Allah I admire (who, what and why)...

I am grateful (to, for, to have)...

Continue
being thankful
and the BLESSING
upon you
will
CONTINUE.

IMAM ALI (AS)

MORNING

I am feeling...

Insha'Allah I will make the next few days great by...

EVENING

Three Alhamdulillah moments...

Three things that made me smile the past few days...

I acted on my chosen value this week by....

MORNING

I am feeling...

My chosen value and how I will act upon it this week...

EVENING

Three Alhamdulillah moments...

What matters today and/or the next few days...

I appreciate about myself...

{task time*}*

I
REMEMBER
YOU...

*Make dua for someone today
(and choose someone different
as often as you can).*

*O Allah, bless me with friends who
remember me in their dua's and make
me of those who also remembers others
in my dua.*

MORNING

I am feeling...

Islamic Mindfulness: I will practise Al-muraqabah this week on these days and times....

EVENING

Three Alhamdulillah moments...

Masha'Allah I admire (who, what and why)...

I am grateful (to, for, to have)...

GIVE THANKS TO THE ROCKS IN YOUR LIFE

MORNING

I am feeling...

Insha'Allah I will make the next few days great by...

EVENING

Three Alhamdulillah moments...

Three things that made me smile the past few days...

I acted on my chosen value this week by....

MORNING

I am feeling...

My chosen value and how I will act upon it this week...

EVENING

Three Alhamdulillah moments...

What matters today and/or the next few days...

I appreciate about myself...

"Alhamdulillah
won't circumvent
the heartbreak.
Alhamdulillah
won't ease the pain.
Alhamdulillah
isn't the happy pill.
Alhamdulillah
is simply the act of
cultivating gratitude
and praise in all our
circumstances."

SAMIA

MORNING

I am feeling...

Islamic Mindfulness: I will practise Al-muraqabah this week on these days and times....

EVENING

Three Alhamdulillah moments...

Masha'Allah I admire (who, what and why)...

I am grateful (to, for, to have)...

When some
BLESSINGS
COME
to you,
do not
drive them away
through
thanklessness.

IMAM ALI (AS)

MORNING

I am feeling...

Insha'Allah I will make the next few days great by...

EVENING

Three Alhamdulillah moments...

Three things that made me smile the past few days...

I acted on my chosen value this week by....

MORNING

I am feeling...

My chosen value and how I will act upon it this week...

EVENING

Three Alhamdulillah moments...

What matters today and/or the next few days...

I appreciate about myself...

Who are you thankful to?

I am thankful first to Allah (swt) for this life, for being guided to the straight path, and for my parents, my spouse, my children, my family and friends. I am grateful to my parents for their love, patience and sacrifice in raising me and my siblings.

SHAZIA AHMED,
CANADA

MORNING

I am feeling...

Islamic Mindfulness: I will practise Al-muraqabah this week on these days and times....

EVENING

Three Alhamdulillah moments...

Masha'Allah I admire (who, what and why)...

I am grateful (to, for, to have)...

Thankfulness
is the
VISION of the
BESTOWER,
not the vision of the blessing.

SHIBLI

MORNING

I am feeling...

Insha'Allah I will make the next few days great by...

EVENING

Three Alhamdulillah moments...

Three things that made me smile the past few days...

I acted on my chosen value this week by....

MORNING

I am feeling...

My chosen value and how I will act upon it this week...

EVENING

Three Alhamdulillah moments...

What matters today and/or the next few days...

I appreciate about myself...

{task time*}*

WRITE A LETTER TO YOURSELF

about how you think your life would be
without the things that you are grateful
for today.

MORNING

I am feeling...

Islamic Mindfulness: I will practise Al-muraqabah this week on these days and times....

EVENING

Three Alhamdulillah moments...

Masha'Allah I admire (who, what and why)...

I am grateful (to, for, to have)...

ALLAH
(swt) **IS**
PLEASED

with His servant if when he
eats something
he thanks Allah for it,
and when he
drinks something
he thanks Allah for it.

PROPHET (PBUH) (MUSLIM)

MORNING

I am feeling...

Insha'Allah I will make the next few days great by...

EVENING

Three Alhamdulillah moments...

Three things that made me smile the past few days...

I acted on my chosen value this week by....

MORNING

I am feeling...

My chosen value and how I will act upon it this week...

EVENING

Three Alhamdulillah moments...

What matters today and/or the next few days...

I appreciate about myself...

"What hurts you today will be your source of growth tomorrow. Adversity can help nurture qualities that shape us to become better people. The only catch is you have to feel the pain to get there."

"From the perfection of Allah's ihsan is that He allows His slave to taste the bitterness of the break before the sweetness of the mend. So He does not break his believing slave, except to mend him. And He does not withhold from him, except to give him. And He does not test him (with hardship), except to cure him."

Ibn Qayyim Al-Jawziyyah (RA)

SAMIA

MORNING

I am feeling...

Islamic Mindfulness: I will practise Al-muraqabah this week on these days and times....

EVENING

Three Alhamdulillah moments...

Masha'Allah I admire (who, what and why)...

I am grateful (to, for, to have)...

Fear is *not*
the opposite of hope.
Rather,
it is a
CLOSE
COMPANION to it.

IMAM AL-GHAZALI IN THE IHYA

MORNING

I am feeling...

Insha'Allah I will make the next few days great by...

EVENING

Three Alhamdulillah moments...

Three things that made me smile the past few days...

I acted on my chosen value this week by....

MORNING

I am feeling...

My chosen value and how I will act upon it this week...

EVENING

Three Alhamdulillah moments...

What matters today and/or the next few days...

I appreciate about myself...

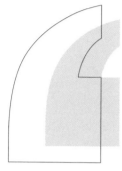

Gratitude,
what is
your why?

My why – To inspire the love of Allah and His Messenger (pbuh) so that our future generations including our children and their children can be proud of their identity as a Muslim, has a strong ummah for support and will hold tight to their deen. Ultimately, everything I do is for the sake of Allah, Insha'Allah.

MAYLENE SEAH, UK

MORNING

I am feeling...

Islamic Mindfulness: I will practise Al-muraqabah this week on these days and times....

EVENING

Three Alhamdulillah moments...

Masha'Allah I admire (who, what and why)...

I am grateful (to, for, to have)...

IT IS HE

Who brought you forth
from the wombs
of your mothers
when you knew nothing; and
*He gave you hearing
and sight
and intelligence
and affection:*
that you may
give thanks (to Allah swt).

AN-NAHL: 78

MORNING

I am feeling...

Insha'Allah I will make the next few days great by...

EVENING

Three Alhamdulillah moments...

Three things that made me smile the past few days...

I acted on my chosen value this week by....

MORNING

I am feeling...

My chosen value and how I will act upon it this week...

EVENING

Three Alhamdulillah moments...

What matters today and/or the next few days...

I appreciate about myself...

{*task* time}

THINK OF A TIME IN YOUR LIFE

when you experienced adversity or difficulty. Make a list of what you learned as an outcome. How has this event shaped you to grow?

"There is no better than adversity. Every defeat, every heartbreak, every loss, contains its own seed, its own lesson on how to improve your performance the next time."
Malcolm X

MORNING

I am feeling...

Islamic Mindfulness: I will practise Al-muraqabah this week on these days and times....

EVENING

Three Alhamdulillah moments...

Masha'Allah I admire (who, what and why)...

I am grateful (to, for, to have)...

To
KNOW
ALLAH (swt)
is to place
your trust
in Him (swt).

MORNING

I am feeling...

Insha'Allah I will make the next few days great by...

EVENING

Three Alhamdulillah moments...

Three things that made me smile the past few days...

I acted on my chosen value this week by....

MORNING

I am feeling...

My chosen value and how I will act upon it this week...

EVENING

Three Alhamdulillah moments...

What matters today and/or the next few days...

I appreciate about myself...

"True love is a gift from Al-Wadud, The Source of Love, He (swt) is the Giver. Love is a rizq, and from whose heart we will receive love is unknown, and for how long. Provisions are just that, provisional gifts from The Giver. Love's longevity is cultivated through care, honour and sustained through Him (swt)."

SAMIA

MORNING

I am feeling...

Islamic Mindfulness: I will practise Al-muraqabah this week on these days and times....

EVENING

Three Alhamdulillah moments...

Masha'Allah I admire (who, what and why)...

I am grateful (to, for, to have)...

Allah (swt)
does not close a door
to His slave,
out of wisdom,
except that
HE OPENS TWO OTHERS
to him.

IBN AL QAYYIM (RA)

MORNING

I am feeling...

Insha'Allah I will make the next few days great by...

EVENING

Three Alhamdulillah moments...

Three things that made me smile the past few days...

I acted on my chosen value this week by....

MORNING

I am feeling...

My chosen value and how I will act upon it this week...

EVENING

Three Alhamdulillah moments...

What matters today and/or the next few days...

I appreciate about myself...

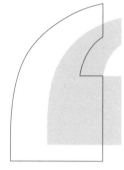

What motivates you to complete your day?

My purpose to make a positive impact from the smallest gesture daily to one day creating my legacy.

ZAHARA MALIK,
UK & UAE

MORNING

I am feeling...

Islamic Mindfulness: I will practise Al-muraqabah this week on these days and times....

EVENING

Three Alhamdulillah moments...

Masha'Allah I admire (who, what and why)...

I am grateful (to, for, to have)...

God (swt) is Kind
and
LIKES
KINDNESS
in *all things.*

THE PROPHET (PBUH)

MORNING

I am feeling...

Insha'Allah I will make the next few days great by...

EVENING

Three Alhamdulillah moments...

Three things that made me smile the past few days...

I acted on my chosen value this week by....

MORNING

I am feeling...

My chosen value and how I will act upon it this week...

EVENING

Three Alhamdulillah moments...

What matters today and/or the next few days...

I appreciate about myself...

"Your present state is
a development of your
past. Your future is a
development of your
present. There is no past.
There is only growth so
embrace change, because
it will happen anyway.
Trust in His (swt) plan,
wherever the journey
leads, amidst the joy
and the difficult turns,
remember Alhamdulillah."

SAMIA

MORNING

I am feeling...

Islamic Mindfulness: I will practise Al-muraqabah this week on these days and times....

EVENING

Three Alhamdulillah moments...

Masha'Allah I admire (who, what and why)...

I am grateful (to, for, to have)...

Know that
GOD (swt)
IS
MORE KIND

to you
than *you are*
to yourself.

IMAM ALI

MORNING

I am feeling...

Insha'Allah I will make the next few days great by...

EVENING

Three Alhamdulillah moments...

Three things that made me smile the past few days...

I acted on my chosen value this week by....

REFLECTION

Self-Evaluation

My Aims, Developments

& Improvements for the Future

My Duas, Hopes & Aspirations

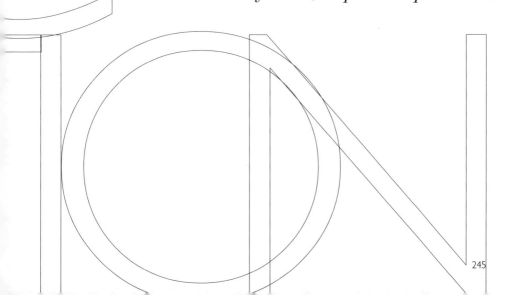

You have come to the end
but your Alhamdulillah journey hasn't.

REFLECTION

One Final...

{task time}

FINAL REFLECTIVE LETTER

From the list compiled on page 132, select one person to write a letter of gratitude to. Tell them why they are important to you and how they make your life better. Think about what your life would be like without their presence.

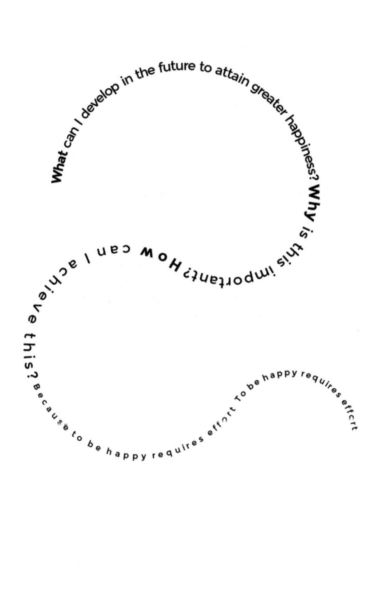

What can I develop in the future to attain greater happiness? Why is this important? How can I achieve this? Because to be happy requires effort To be happy requires effort

Self-Evaluation

Have you achieved Taqdeer's aims?

1   **Relay** gratitude of blessings to Allah (swt)
through a consistent and reflective approach   YES / NO

2   **Remember** Allah (swt) at the start, during,
and end of each day, every day   YES / NO

3   **Improve** self-awareness of
the positives in your life   YES / NO

4   **Focus** on days, events and experiences
from a perspective of gratitude   YES / NO

5   **Contemplate** how you can put
your blessings to good use   YES / NO

6   **Record** current positive happenings that can at
times be easily missed or clouded by challenging
events as well as reflecting on the blessings
arising from these difficult times   YES / NO

7   **Monitor** and establish patterns that have triggered
the act of gratitude for future self-reflection   YES / NO

8   **Develop** what is within your capacity to shape
your future to reach a state of increased
happiness and positive well-being   YES / NO

My Aims, Developments & Improvements for the Future

My Duas, Hopes & Aspirations

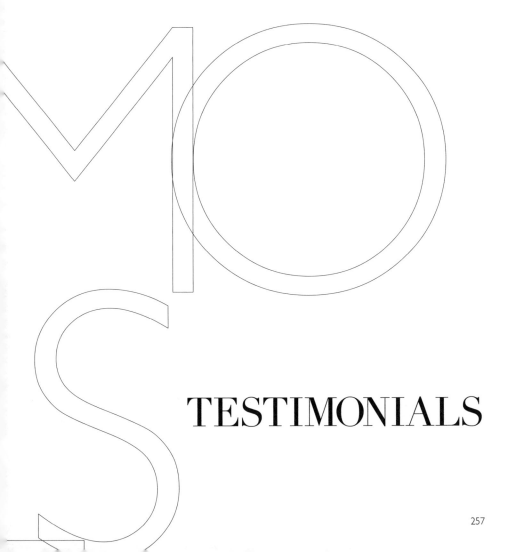

TESTIMONIALS

What some members of our Taqdeer Life family say about our journal...

'My friend Rumana gave me the journal as a gift. Although I am not Muslim, I am spiritual and I do like being able to reflect on my life and this is a great way of doing it. I like the fact that I am able to focus on the positives in life and identify what I am grateful for. I have suffered with depression and although I am in a good place now, the Taqdeer journal allows me to keep a positive frame of mind and appreciation for what I have. It's nice to read back on what I have written especially when I am feeling low or having a bad day because I can take the focus off the negatives. I would definitely recommend it.' *Rosie McBooth*

'In love with this gratitude journal. Actually it's so much more than a regular gratitude journal. It includes space to write about feelings, inspirations, needs and motivations to perform good deeds. Epitome of Islam-inspired self-care.' *Ashiya*

"Thank you for acknowledging a huge gap in the market and for creating something so powerful yet so simple." *Zainab Pandhair*

'I've got to say I've always been sceptical about gratitude journals etc (think it's the staunch Yorkshire person in me all about logic and practicality!). But loved the concept of one that is connected to my faith. I bought one a few months ago and though on some days I feel like I've had a bad day mentally really makes you stop and flip thinking to what Allah (swt) provided me with today to be grateful for.' *Railla Razaq*

'We've been working on a page a day Alhamdulillah taking the time to reflect, appreciate and contemplate. It's proving to be so useful not just as mother and daughter time but as a family, Alhamdulillah looking forward to carrying on.' *Fatima Shikora*

'I gifted the journal to my revert friend. As an undergrad Psychology student, the journal is the perfect way for her to write about her first year experiences as a Muslim. Insha'Allah the reflection will help to increase and strengthen her Imaan. The Adhkaar in the journal will be invaluable! I make dua the Taqdeer journal remains a sadaqah jariyah for you till the end of time.' *Arifah*

'Started using your diary last week. Best self-reflection exercises I have ever done. Going through a confusing time of my life but I absolutely feel so much more content and optimistic when I'm reflecting on good things that happened through the week using your diary's reflection prompts. Well done your work of art is beauts! I've gotten one for my cousin, I think she'll love it too.' *Shazia*

'Just wanted to let you know how much I'm enjoying your journal. Full of goodness and thoroughly thought out as well and put together smartly Masha'Allah. Thank you for sharing this with us, its much needed in our Muslim Ummah.' *Eymaan Rayes*

'My husband got this for me as a gift - it's beautiful- can't wait to start writing. My father recently passed away and it feels like the right time to start journaling.' **Shafeen**

'The reason behind buying this diary is I lost my mother eight months ago, which has turned my life upside down but I'm trying to make sense in it all and trust in Allah (swt)'s plan for us all. I'm trying to hold onto the little moments of happiness I feel everyday and I'm the type of person who writes everything down so this is perfect for me. It's sad that we have to go through something tragic to realise what's important in life. Alhumdulilah for everything. Thank you for creating this.' **N.M.**

HOW DID YOU FIND TAQDEER?
We would love to know about your experience, feedback and thoughts at salaam@taqdeer.life

REFERENCE

Gratitude | Bibliography

Gratitude

Derived from the Quran and the work of spiritual theologians, this section provides a comprehensive reference to thankfulness/Shukr related sayings.

"Imaan is of two halves; half is patience (Sabr) and the other half is being thankful (Shukr)."
Ibn Qayyim Al-Jawziyya

"Thus do We reward he who is grateful."
Al-Qamar: 35

"Whoever is not grateful to the people, he is not grateful to Allah."
Tirmidhi

The Prophet (pbuh) said, "Whoever does not thank people has not thanked Allah."
Abu Huraira (as)

"And who is grateful, does so to the profit of his own soul."
Al-Luqman: 12

The Prophet (pbuh) said, "A grateful eater will have a reward like that of a patient fasting person."
Ibn Majah

"... and be grateful to Allah, if it is Him you worship."
Al-Baqarah: 172

"Blessings are connected to gratitude, and gratitude leads to more blessings, they are attracted to one another."
Ali ibn Abi Talib

"Continue being thankful and the blessing upon you will continue."
Imam Ali (as)

"It is He Who brought you forth from the wombs of your mothers when you knew nothing; and He gave you hearing and sight and intelligence and affection: that you may give thanks (to Allah)."
An-Nahl: 78

"Showing gratitude to Your Lord is done through prolonged praise."
Imam Ali (as)

"If you are grateful, He is pleased with you..."
Az-Zumar: 7

"Allah is pleased with His servant if, when he eats something, he thanks Allah for it, and when he drinks something, he thanks Allah for it."
The Prophet (pbuh) (Muslim)

"When some blessings come to you, do not drive them away through thanklessness."
Imam Ali (as)

"Allah will reward the grateful."
Al-Imran: 144

"If you are grateful, I will surely give you more and more."
Ibrahim: 7

"Thankfulness is the vision of the Bestower, not the vision of the blessing."
Shibli

"And He made me blessed wherever I am."
Maryam: 31

"And whatever of blessings and good things you have, it is from Allah."
An-Nahl: 53

"Know that thankfulness is from the highest of stations, and it is higher than patience and fear and detachment of the world."
Imam Al Ghazali

"Therefore remember Me (by praying, glorifying). I will remember you, and be grateful to Me (for My countless favours on you) and never be ungrateful to Me."
Al-Baqarah: 152

"If we had perfect power to determine our destinies; and perfect vision to see the future and know what is best for us, we would choose exactly the fate that Allah has chosen for us."
Imam Al-Ghazali

"How wonderful is the case of a Believer. There is good for him in whatever happens to him -and none, apart from him, enjoys this blessing. If he receives some bounty, he is grateful to Allah and this bounty brings good to him. And if some adversity befalls him, he is patient, and this affliction, too, brings good to him."
The Prophet (pbuh) (Muslim)

"Allah, whatever blessing has been received by me or anyone of Your creation is from You alone. You have no partner. All praise is for You and thanks is to You."
(Adhkar)

"If you tried to count Allah's blessings, you would never be able to number them."
Ibrahim: 34

"Among the faults of the soul is obliviousness to blessings."
Imam Mawlud

"Whoever among you wakes up physically healthy, feeling safe and secure within himself, with food for the day, it is as if he acquired the whole world."
Ibn Majah

"Allah loves to see the traces of blessings on his servant."
Al Mu'Jam Al-Kabir

"Talk about the blessings of your Lord."
Al-Duha: 11

"Oh Allah, help me remember you, thank you and worship You beautifully."
Prophet (pbuh)

"To protect your blessings utter:"Ma sha Allahu la quwata illa billa" (As Allah wishes – there is no power except by Allah)"
Ibn Sunni

"Allah's Generosity is connected to gratitude, and gratitude is linked to increase in His (swt) generosity. The generosity of Allah will not stop increasing unless the gratitude of the servant ceases."
Ali Ibn Abi-Talib

"Be grateful for your life, every detail of it, and your face will come to shine like a sun and everyone who sees it will be made glad and peaceful."
Rumi

"There is no one who is happy except he experiences sadness, therefore attain your happiness by showing gratitude and render your sadness into patience."
Imam al-Baghawi

SHUKR CAN BE SHOWN IN THREE WAYS:

Shukr of the heart (Qalb), which is achieved by intending good for all of Allah (swt)'s creation.

Shukr of the tongue (Lisan), uttering Alhamdulillah, and expressing gratefulness vocally.

Shukr of actions (Jawarih), demonstrating thanks to Allah (swt) by carrying out pleasing, righteous deeds that are in service to others.

Bibliography

Achor, S. (2011)
The Happiness Advantage: The Seven Principles that Fuel
Success and Performance at Work

Adler, M. G., & Fagley, N. S. (2005)
Appreciation: Individual differences in finding value and meaning
as a unique predictor of subjective well-being

Al-Ashkar, U.S. (2003)
The World of The Noble Angels. IIPH

Al-Qahtani, S.
Fortification of the Muslim through remembrance and supplication
from the Qur'aan and Sunnah

Al-Seheel, A.Y and Noor, N.M. (2016)
Effects of an Islamic-based gratitude strategy on Muslim students'
level of happiness

Aplin, O. (2017)
Why Men Should Keep a Journal The Guardian

Aqababaii, N., Farahani, H., & Tabik, M.T. (2012)
The relationship between gratitude to God, personality, well-
being and mental health factors

Armstrong, K. (2011)
Twelve steps to a compassionate heart

Barker, E. (2016)
Doing These 4 Things Will Make You Happier, According to Neuroscience. Motto TIME

Barak, Y. (2006)
The Immune System and Happiness

Bion, W. (1970)
Container and Contained: Attention and Interpretation. London: Tavistock

Blurt Team (2018)
How bullet journaling can help us manage our mental health

Greater Good in Action Science-based Practices for a Meaningful Life. Three Good Things. The Greater Good Science Centre at The University of Berkeley
https://greatergood.berkeley.edu

The Greater Good Science Centre at The University of Berkeley (2018)
The Science of Gratitude

The Greater Good Science Centre at The University of Berkeley (2014)
The Science of Happiness

Kamen, Dr. R (2015)
The Transformative Power of Gratitude. Huffpost

Kershavarzi H, Haque, A. (2013)
Outlining a Psychotherapy Model for Enhancing Muslim Mental Health within an Islamic Context

Living, O. (2015)
The Science Behind Why Naming Our Feelings Makes Us Happier

Lyubomirsky, S., Sheldon, K. M., & Schkade, D. (2005)
Pursuing happiness: The architecture of sustainable change

Lyubomirsky, S. (2008)
The How of Happiness

Macmillan, A. (2017)
Being Generous Really Does Make You Happier. TIME Health

Otake, K., Shimai, S., Tanaka-Matsumi, J., Otsui, K., & Fredrickson, B. L. (2006)
Happy people become happier through kindness: A counting kindness intervention

Parrott, J. (2018)
How to be a mindful Muslim: an exercise in Islamic meditation. US: Yaqeen Institute. https://yaqeeninstitute.org/ justin-parrott/how-to-be-a-mindfulmuslim-an-exercise-in-islamicmeditation/#.XRyowi2Q2t8

Pennebaker, J. W. and Smyth, J.M. (2016)
Opening Up by Writing It Down

Quddus, S. (2020)
Trust in Allah, but tie your camel. BACP Children, Young People and Families, March: p16-19

Rosmarin, D. H., Pirutinsky, S., Cohen, A., Galler, Y., & Krumrei, E. J. (2011)
Grateful to God or just plain grateful? A study of religious and non-religious gratitude

Schwartz, T. (2015)
The Importance of Naming Your Emotions. The New York Times

Sheldon, K. M., & Lyubomirsky, S. (2006)
How to increase and sustain positive emotion: The effects of expressing gratitude and visualizing best possible selves

Siegel, D.J. (2011)
The Whole Brain Child

Skinner, R. (2010)
An Islamic Approach to Psychology and Mental Health, Religion & Culture

University of California - Los Angeles. (2007)
Putting Feelings Into Words Produces Therapeutic Effects In The Brain. ScienceDaily

This is less like an ending,
rather just another starting point.

Remember to order your next copy
at www.taqdeer.life

HOW DID YOU FIND TAQDEER?
We would love to know about your experience,
feedback and thoughts at salaam@taqdeer.life